FOREVER

YOUNG

by Bob Dylan

Illustrated by Paul Rogers

ginee seo books
Atheneum Books for Young Readers
New York London Toronto Sydney

May God bless and keep you always,

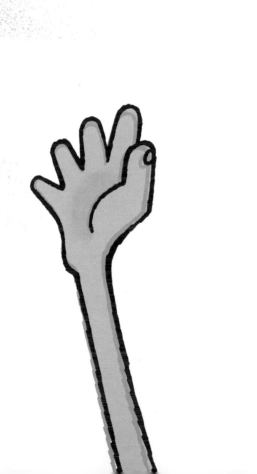

May your wishes all come true,

May you always do for others

And let others do for you.

May you build a ladder to the stars

And climb on every rung,

May you stay forever young,
Forever young, forever young,
May you stay forever young.

May you grow up to be righteous,

May you grow up to be true,

May you always know the truth

And see the lights surrounding you.

May you always be courageous,
Stand upright and be strong,

May you stay forever young,
Forever young, forever young,
May you stay forever young.

May your hands always be busy,
May your feet always be swift,

May you have a strong foundation
When the winds of changes shift.

May your heart always be joyful, May your song always be sung,

May you stay forever young,
Forever young, forever young,
May you stay . . .

forever young.

ILLUSTRATOR'S NOTES

Listening to nearly every Dylan album while creating the illustrations for this book gave me time to think about the people who inspired him and how his music has inspired so many. These drawings include images from Dylan's life and lyrics to his songs. Some are obvious and others are meant to be a bit of a mystery. Here's a list of some of the hidden things you may not have seen the first time you looked at this book. It doesn't include everything – that would spoil the fun of discovering them for yourself. So get some Dylan albums (my son Nate recommends *Blonde On Blonde*, 1966), sit down, listen to the lyrics, look at the book, and see what you can find.

The folksinger playing the guitar is a reference to the great Woody Guthrie, and so is the small sticker on his guitar case. He's in New York, playing on the sidewalk in front of Gerde's Folk City, the legendary folk music club where a young Bob Dylan had some early success. The tambourine on the ground is a reminder of the song "Mr Tambourine Man."

There's an old country music tradition of giving someone your guitar as an act of friendship and admiration. Johnny Cash gave Dylan his guitar when the two met at the Newport Folk Festival in 1963. That's a Siamese cat from "Like a Rolling Stone", keeping an eye on things, but you probably already noticed that.

Stacked against the hi-fi are some records by Woody Guthrie and also one by the underrated Ricky Nelson.

The crowd in the park includes John Hammond, who signed Dylan to his first recording contract; he's the guy holding a copy of Dylan's debut album, *Bob Dylan* (1962). Also listening is the great folksinger Pete Seeger, with a red tie on, and Albert Grossman, Dylan's manager from the early days, wearing a navy blazer. That's Maggie's Ma in a "Leopard-Skin Pillbox Hat" and Joan Baez is clapping along too (she recorded a beautiful version of "Forever Young" in 1976).

Here's a scene in Greenwich Village, the New York neighbourhood that's always been a centre of artistic energy. Café Wha? is where Dylan played on the first night he arrived in New York. The Gaslight Café was also an important spot for his early performances. Folk historian Izzy Young can be seen typing away through the window of the Folklore Centre, and Bob's old friend Dave Van Ronk is playing at Gerde's Folk City. There's a big brass bed in an upstairs window, and the VW bus and old Chevy from the cover of *The Freewheelin' Bob Dylan* (1963) are still parked on Jones Street.

This would be a good time to listen to "Shooting Star" from *Oh Mercy* (1989).

In the '60s there was a street vendor in New York who sold records from a bicycle he rigged to hold his inventory. He's set up shop here on 4th Street ("Positively 4th Street"), and he has a nice selection of records that include Johnny Cash, Robert Johnson, and Blind Willie McTell. This street is not "Desolation Row," but "[t]he beauty parlor is full of sailors / [t]he circus is in town." Search for the "Bob Dylan Bathe My Bird" video on YouTube, and while you're there, also check out "Subterranean Homesick Blues."

On the door is Milton Glaser's poster from *Bob Dylan's Greatest Hits* (1967). The bookshelf is stacked with books that every kid should read, and on the wall are portraits of Cisco Houston, Sonny Terry, and Leadbelly, all mentioned in Dylan's "Song to Woody." The picture of the guy in the red jacket is the actor James Dean.

Washington Square Park, where "dogs run free." Waiting in line to sign the petition are three famous denizens of Greenwich Village, the Beat generation writers Allen Ginsberg, Jack Kerouac (with suitcase), and William Burroughs.

The cardboard box of tapes looks like it came from a basement, and you should look for *The Basement Tapes* (1975), which Dylan recorded with the Band. Look closely—Renaldo and Clara sat under that tree (*Renaldo and Clara* is the title of a movie Dylan made in 1975). The little girl's T-shirt is the same as Bob's on the cover on *Highway 61 Revisited* (1965).

Highway 61 Revisited (1965) is a great album to listen to when you're on the road—or not.

Joining the march are Martin Luther King Jr., Joan Baez, Hank Williams, Albert Einstein, Edie Sedgwick, John Lennon, Thelonious Monk, Peter Blake, Paul McCartney, Ben Shahn, George Harrison, DA Pennebaker, Ringo Starr, and friends.

"Maggie's Farm" is the name of the first song Dylan played when he went electric at the Newport Folk Festival in 1965. Check out the name of the corner pawnshop with the electric guitars in the window.

The question on the sign is taken from "Blowin' in the Wind." In the *Los Angeles Times* in 2004, Dylan discussed the song and said, "I wrote 'Blowin' in the Wind' in ten minutes, just put words to an old spiritual, probably something I learned from Carter Family records. That's the folk tradition. You use what's been handed down"—and, of course, pass it on.

Atheneum Books for Young Readers

An imprint of Simon & Schuster Children's Publishing Division

1230 Avenue of the Americas, New York, New York 10020

Book design by Jill von Hartmann

The text for this book is set in Clarendon.

The illustrations for this book are rendered in ink, acrylic, and Adobe Illustrator.

Manufactured in the United States of America

First Edition

10 9 8 7 6 5 4 3 2 1

CIP data for this book is available from the Library of Congress.

ISBN-13: 978-1-4169-5808-6

ISBN-10: 1-4169-5808-8

For Alex, Nate, and Jill (and in memory of Louis, forever young)

— P. R.

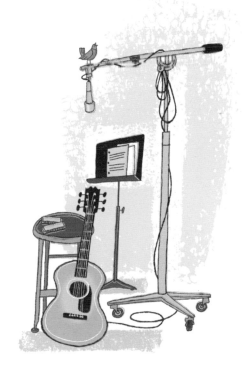